The Mt. Sinai Poems

BY ERIK VATNE

Poetry

CXX Epistles (forthcoming)
Pulaski Skyway & Other Poems (forthcoming 2013)
The Mt. Sinai Poems
X Sonnets (forthcoming)
Words in Search of a Meaning
Mormon Heroin
Dun Scotus on His Sickbed
XXIII Epistles
Cartographies of Silence
Endings

Visual/Performance

The Lovers (2012) 5 minutes, from series of 23 short films

Cartographies of Silence: performance/reading with music by Cliff Thompson (You Tube) at Bowery Poetry Club, August, 2010

Hydra: 40 Drawings

Psychopathia Sexualis (paintings)

32 Italian Verbs: Works-on-Paper (forthcoming)

The S.B. Notebooks: Volumes I-XX (forthcoming) (visual phenomena)

GARAGE: Photographies (forthcoming)

Crossing the Saugatuck: Drawings, Photographies & Poems (forthcoming)

The Mt. Sinai Poems

Erik Vatne

BURNING
APPLE
PRESS

Published by Burning Apple Press
110 Chestnut Ridge Road
#166
Montvale, NJ 07645
E-mail: burningapplepress@hotmail.com

Front and back cover collage: Dylan Thompson
        Based on concept by Erik Vatne
Typeset: Liza Littlefield
        lizalittlefield.com, liza.littlefield@yahoo.com
Back cover photo: Self-Portrait, 2012

These poems were composed from 2008 to 2013.

Thanks to Sanjay Agnihotri and the editors at *Local Knowledge* where some of these poems first appeared.

Thanks to Liza, Dylan, Joseph, Dr. M and family & friends.

Library of Congress Cataloging-in-Publication Data

Vatne, Erik
Poems
ISBN: 0615913105

Manufactured in the United States of America

For Brendan

"The tendency to split means that parts of the psyche detach themselves from consciousness to such an extent that they not only appear foreign but lead an autonomous life of their own."

~Carl Jung

"Every disease is a musical problem; every cure is a musical solution."

~Novalis

The Mt. Sinai Poems

CONTENTS

I

Doc, I'm abt to make a mistake
by opening my mouth:
the poem is NOT a police report
the wing of paranoia
brushed yr black coat w/ snow
y blue wings;
the language plunge a plume
of smoke & feather
y light whispering its ash
into the ear of my mouth

II

Doc, I rent myself out to the other side of this misstep
The way a bridge separates us is
Ghost-text dragged from one country
To the next: I rent myself out to the Renal Mercies:
Renal angels & Evel Knievel actions figure
s high-jump Over hills & vales;
I'll eke out of my salmon skin
My Saint Jerome skull & stuffed grosbeak
Song an aspirin moon
I meant to fizzle insofar as this is possible

III

Doc, I shimmy-shimmy Coco-Pop
UP art-book psycho-Babel bullshit
STOP sign on his forehead
Blinks pink & blue Irish neon
Light Naples under 8-ball siege
I is always before E in his name
Don't stop to think what
Yr going to say Next:
Yes!   You have yr Self
A structure in which to Fail

IV

Doc, I'm just moseying along
minding my own business
when whammo!
I get whacked on the noggin
by these bird's wings
spluttering in my jammed
Throat-wave-radio...
choke
Hey, batter, batter, batter...
Either quay I'm gonna get down
to knit & make marry to Medici Princess

V

Doc, the flesh-house is a black hole;
the sound pours purrs into it—
I play keep-away w/ my own head,
lopped off last nacht in the language-game
of yr dream:
I am NOT a dictionary.
I am fiction.
I sound my way into things
& out of things
I am sounded

VI

Doc, I weave the event into act to tell song
Watt 2 feel: why could nut
Get that oolong into my mouth-store
Aped for you to organ size into phlox
Sized bites—something abt this Vision
Requires requiems: example:
Thereissomuchmoretosay...
 Yr preview of watts next in sequence
Where the rubber meets the road
This is the last time I step on yr squeeze toy

VII

Doc, I continue to scan
the window-movie
for additional narrative
addenda—of course
it's crazy to talk gobbledygook
in the high room, while
others needle words into
Theremins & apostates
of rainy pleasure. You pluck
this music from my hand
like a mealy apple
after the first
Frost

VIII

Doc, eluvia elusive because I'm tryin' to hide
something   I outloved them
why I lived in the voice-room
episodic series storyboard the love scene;
clumps of okra   I don't feel
I know howdah have fun no more:
I remember funhouse mirror dis-
torsion of aggregates   What is the Greek
Root for Grace?   The eyes that satyr
back at me w/ my father's demons

IX

Doc, I need to look
in yr medical dictionary
to hear the birds jargon
⟦the jargon of the birds⟧
in the doc's black medical
bag where he plays keep-
away w/ my head
& the page we're looking for
is missing from the
Lexical scale of lost languages

X

Doc, never saw no birds where I grew up
Didn't hear a sound
Never _____
I'm 'fraid to lookat what I rote last nacht
No body looks rights like that
He just liked the way it sounds in mind's-ear
& looks on papyrus
Below: black feathers flapping in snow
Where am i? lost?   Why do this to my-
Self?   Why didn't you do WHAT2OTHER?
To make her a mix-tape of our love soundtrack

XI

Doc, I don't know watt to talk abt any more
the parallel o gram of Afghan grains in spoon
God-wise are welcome maps reliefs from lieder;
it's Lent again but I'm a quitter all ready
the need to be write & roll up
the sleeve of the record if the disc is slipped
into like a sonar eclipse above the Sphinx
I outloved the lunar moth of her smile
fluttering in a Staten Island promenade
Breeze

XII

Doc, I'm a lazy language man:
My wives & mothers play Monkey-in-the-Middle
w/ my Lyfe: there are 2 too many women
& know enuf Eternity in the chewy nougat centre
of my skull: sit still for a while & wait...
I outloved them: it's WHY I live in the voice-room
Design & story-board episodic love scenes w/
Snow-globes of Reykjavik & Venice
I shake out the artificial snowy static of love
Until it settles to the bottom of the glass

XIII

Doc, there were no more bicycles
in Beijing: the lovers clutched
each other on the unmade bed:
they were perennials; in transit.
Upside the hotel
The cars pilled up as the lovebirds
were towed out in body bags
fire rained down from the grey sky
like a musical that closes on opening nacht
or a kraut porn-flick dubbed into Latin
I hovered over Echo Park

XIV

Doc, he leaves them wanting more...
Light, as Goethe cried: ...
The wren they purred into the poem
little whips: wisps of smoke perfectly spent
gauged lingua shotgun blasts like elephant road kill eaten by
hyenas
Quan Yin pours the vessel
& Lux drains into the hole in his skull
& down the throat-song-saliva-orb swallowed
"Touche-moi de ta salive..."
Vesicles of mixed elixir like a nozzle to God
Faith in what is left after the beforebirth

XV

Doc, don't try & psyche me out w/
yr card tricks in that black bag
you stole from Felix: I got language
to harangue & ague shiver in Shiva spine
like eel fever blues   windows
to Thor too open & leap out of
into the tricky light
I outloved the raison excreta
of my Lyfe   Words
are shuffled & the game is forgotten
Do you wanna play 52- pickup?

XVI

Doc, what is the name of that bird
that chirps at nacht? The one that doesn't
STOP humming itself silly w/ acetate recordings
by Bix Beiderbecke? It don't sing the blues;
it's just cuckoo—and ain't that a substitute for
REAL suffering according to my father Carl Jung—
Redundant & flame-retardant pajamas were on fire
as we leapt into kidney shaped pools of blood
in Berlin. Abracadabra & it all makes sense now:
WHAT was the name of that man in the dream?
that hummed inside the secret language of Ssh...

XVII

Doc, I am swept up in the pituitary swoop
of bird-song! Flashing splotches of blue & red:
what description of these variations can't contain
in the primal soup. I hear the whoop & whorl
of canned laughter in the off kilter flying
colours: it's all so sæligas & perfect it hurts:
I am NOT going to calm down! I am NOT going
to 'get a grip on myself!' oh let me bliss my-Self
Forever in the language plume of their open wings
where even the pharmacies of feathers never close!

XVIII

Doc, I don't know watt 2 do
abt the Hindi butter word
singing outside my window?
I don't remember the ear-eye
Sign instructions we inherited
from the dead—but intense feelings
of heat & lust drag me deeper
into an understanding of that terror:
I know what it means.
I have lugged it in this flesh-house my Lyfe.

XIX

Doc, I gotta karaoke the Core of my Heart
song to get well—even if I don`t want to get well—
while the war rages outside & men`s arms & legs
are blown off & standing at my bedside is that beautiful
Swiss nurse holding my hand—while my buddies
are in hell—and in here I can be Spirit & bird-song—
it blushes blue & red like a residue of damp wampum
in the chocolate screed of summer—to feel it better—
bigger & more of—camouflage code in secret insignia
letter—like igloo chum—I made this form you—
a pudding from the skull-scoop of memories
& ME—that ~~eudemon~~ Eidolon of amnesia

XX

Doc, I will invent you as my Fuhrer:
3 drops of colloidal silver under my tongue—
the words hide in the culvert ravine duct-tape
Scranton, Pennsylvania   or do we reinvent applause
as the band warms up backstage
1 2 3 4 5 6 7 8 9
= no one could get away w/ that N O W:
not a snowball's chance in Poughkeepsie such psalms
shd be lifted   like Ezekiel   l i f t e d
afloat   has l i f e   in IT
...but chough's it up counterclockwise fire
reminds us our   T I M E   is   UP

XXI

Doc, I got all these femurs feelings
I don't know what to do with—each aggregate
of bird-egg cracking open into stony epoch
makes me hug my knees & rock back & forth
ion in the baton-train—when what I need is
walking- medicine—outer levels pivot on ossified
sentries that is as lost as we are in the tooth whistle
 Q   drinks Nyquil before beddy-bye river boat
Down Nile w/ Koko Taylor singin' Wang Dang
Doodle all night long I whittled the ivory elephant
& it floated away in the Nile air in search of Her

XXII

Doc, I was in & out of consciousness for many lives.
I was gate-crashing the loony tunes lunar vision
& exercised each ear-ache of body-window-wisdom
for the Saint fodder in archival snuff films of my Lyfe
playing radar w/ my little scarps scraps of arroyo paper
to remind me of H O M E where the Black Communion
Box waits to swallow me up like Jonah in the whale's belly
While the little boy waits his turn for that wafer of Light
Do you see how inside every step on the language ladder
leads back to the bird-song in the no-go-zone of the heart?
I am re-envisioning my inner histories as we speak...

ABOUT THE AUTHOR

Erik Vatne is a poet and multi-disciplinary artist born and raised in New Jersey. He holds degrees from Bard College and Trinity College Dublin. He has published seven collections of poetry, including *Cartographies of Silence* (2009, Station Hill Press) and the 400+ page book of poems, *Mormon Heroin* (2012).

His poems have appeared in many print and online journals and his poems have been translated into Greek and were included in the world-anthology of poetry edited by Yanni Livadas, *35 Poets*. He has been shortlisted for the Strokestown International Poetry Award (Ireland) and the Philadelphia City Paper Poetry Prize. He is currently working on a multimedia project called *Crossing the Saugatuck*.

The text was set in Kennerly 12 point. This edition consists of 500 copies of which 26 are numbered and signed by the author.

www.ingramcontent.com/pod-product-compliance
Lightning Source LLC
Chambersburg PA
CBHW022349040426
42449CB00006B/790